CENGAGE Learning

Novels for Students, Volume 6

Staff

Series Editors: Marie Rose Napierkowski and Deborah A. Stanley.

Contributing Editors: Betsy Currier Beacom, Robert Bennett, Karen R. Bloom, Chloe Bolan, Sara L. Constantakis, Sharon Cumberland, Carl Davis, Jane Elizabeth Dougherty, Scott Gillam, Catherine L. Goldstein, Margaret Haerens, Jhan Hochman, Jeremy Hubbell, Motoko Fujishiro Huthwaite, Arlene M. Johnson, David Kelly, Paul Loeber, Nancy C. McClure, Tabitha McIntosh-Byrd, Patrick J. Moser, Wendy Perkins, Diane Telgen, Beverly West, and Donna Woodford.

Editorial Technical Specialist: Karen Uchic.

Managing Editor: Joyce Nakamura.

Research: Victoria B. Cariappa, *Research Team Manager*. Andy Malonis, *Research Specialist*. Julia

C. Daniel, Tamara C. Nott, Tracie A. Richardson, and Cheryl L. Warnock, *Research Associates*. Jeffrey Daniels, *Research Assistant*.

Permissions: Susan M. Trosky, *Permissions Manager*. Maria L. Franklin, *Permissions Specialist*. Sarah Chesney, *Permissions Associate*.

Production: Mary Beth Trimper, *Production Director*. Evi Seoud, *Assistant Production Manager*. Cindy Range, *Production Assistant*.

Graphic Services: Randy Bassett, *Image Database Supervisor*. Robert Duncan and Michael Logusz, *Imaging Specialists*. Pamela A. Reed, *Photography Coordinator*. Gary Leach, *Macintosh Artist*.

Product Design: Cynthia Baldwin, *Product Design Manager*. Cover Design: Michelle DiMercurio, *Art Director*. Page Design: Pamela A. E. Galbreath, *Senior Art Director*.

Copyright Notice

individual does not imply endorsement of the editors or publisher. Errors brought to the attention of the publisher and verified to the satisfaction of the publisher will be corrected in future editions.

Gale Research
27500 Drake Rd.
Farmington Hills, MI 48331-3535

ISBN 0-7876-2115-3
ISSN 1094-3552

One Day in the Life of Ivan Denisovich

Aleksandr Solzhenitsyn

1963

Introduction

Aleksandr Solzhenitsyn secretly wrote *One Day in the Life of Ivan Denisovich* during the Cold War, an era during which the Union of Soviet Socialist Republics (USSR) and the United States, the world's superpowers, fought each other psychologically by stockpiling more and more destructive weapons in preparation for a real and possibly world-ending war. One of the few confidants Solzhenitsyn allowed to read his novel said, "There are now three atomic bombs in the world. The White House has one, the Kremlin the second—and you the third" (quoted in David Burg and George Feifer's *Solzhenitsyn*).

When the Twenty-second Congress met in 1961, Nikita Khrushchev defamed Stalin's tyrannical excesses, explaining that they were due to "the cult of personality," and promised they would never again be allowed. Afterwards Stalin's body was removed from Red Square and cremated. The political fire needed to detonate Solzhenitsyn's bomb had been set.

Solzhenitsyn brought his work to the liberal magazine *Novy Mir*. Its famous editor, Aleksandr Tvardovsky, showed it to Khrushchev, who approved its publication. Every copy of the magazine was sold, and each buyer had a long list of friends anxious to read it as well. A second and last printing followed and was immediately sold out. Western publishers acquired the manuscript, and, since the Soviets did not observe international copyright laws, were free to publish translations without the author's approval. The quality of these translations varied from good to mediocre. Still, the literary merits of the novel with its unities of time and place—one day in a forced-labor camp—and its common-man protagonist accepting his situation without self-pity were clear. However, because of its content, any literary evaluation would be eclipsed by its political importance in disclosing the dark past of Stalinism. Solzhenitsyn's subsequent works continued this exposure.

Author Biography

Aleksandr Solzhenitsyn was born on December 11, 1918, in Kislovodsk, Russia. His father, an artillery officer in World War I, died in an accident before he was born, and his mother raised him on a secretary's salary. He studied mathematics at the University of Rostov and graduated in 1941, after having married fellow student Natalya Reshetovskaya in 1940. He became an artillery officer in the Soviet Army during World War II and was decorated twice for valor. However, in letters to a friend he criticized the dictator Josef Stalin, referring to him indirectly as "the whiskered one" or "the boss" in Yiddish. This led to his being stripped of his rank and medals and sentenced to a Moscow prison. He spent the last four years of his eight-year sentence at a forced-labor camp in Kazakhstan, where he conceived *One Day in the Life of Ivan Denisovich*. During this period he also underwent a cancer operation and his wife was forced to divorce him. When he was finally freed, he was not allowed to return home, but instead was required to stay in Kazakhstan. He taught mathematics and wrote "underground," meaning he kept his writing a secret and hid the papers he wrote for fear of discovery by the KGB, the secret police.

Solzhenitsyn didn't expect his work to be published; he wrote because he had to tell the truth about life in the Soviet Union. However, in 1962, the political climate changed briefly. Premiere

Nikita Khrushchev wanted to denounce his predecessor, Josef Stalin, so Solzhenitsyn exposed his underground book to the editors of *Novy Mir*, a liberal magazine. His novella was published, but it soon led to trouble for Solzhenitsyn. Khrushchev fell and the "Iron Curtain" of Soviet secrets shut tightly again. Solzhenitsyn then had to battle the Soviet Writers Union, an organization whose purpose was to publish only those writers who adhered to Socialist Realism, a style that supports and even glorifies the Communist party line. But the world had its glimpse of the real Soviet Union, thanks to Solzhenitsyn, and that vision would not fade; in fact, it would intensify. Although Solzhenitsyn's future writings weren't printed in Russia, they were published in the West. *One Day*, along with *The First Circle* and *Cancer Ward*, earned Solzhenitsyn the Nobel Prize in 1970.

In 1974, the KGB struck and Solzhenitsyn was exiled from Russia while in the process of publishing *The Gulag Archipelago*. He moved to Vermont in the United States with his second wife and children, where he stayed until the political climate changed again. The Soviet Union collapsed, and in 1994 Solzhenitsyn, who some consider to be the conscience of Russia, returned to his homeland.

"Reveille was sounded, as always, at 5 A.M....."

So begins another day for Ivan Denisovich in a forced labor camp in Siberia, in a pitch-dark room filled with two hundred men, stacked four bunks high. Usually he gets up and finds one of the numerous ways to earn more food, but this morning he's sick. Not sick enough to know he can't work, but sick enough to wonder if he can. He plans on going to the infirmary, but a mean guard, the thin Tartar, catches him in his bunk and sentences him to solitary confinement for three days. Fortunately for Ivan, he only has him mop the floor of the warders' office. Inside the warders check the thermometer. If it is lower than forty below zero, the men won't have to work outside. It registers sixteen degrees below, but the men know it isn't accurate and there's no talk of fixing it. Ivan does a poor job of mopping: "If you're working for human beings, then do a real job of it, but if you work for dopes, then you just go through the motions."

The beginning segment of the novel firmly establishes the prison setting, its unspoken laws, and the goal of the prisoners: to survive. Ivan recalls his former gang boss from another camp who told the men that even though jungle law reigns, certain behavior signals a non-survivor: "the guy who licks out bowls, puts his faith in the infirmary, or squeals to the screws." Another firmly established theme is Ivan's health. Because he starts the day not feeling well, he tracks his health for the rest of the day. His psychological health is closely tied to his physical health. For example, today is the day his gang finds out whether they are to be reassigned to build on an unsheltered area. Since fuel is such a valuable commodity, they won't be able to make a fire. This could spell death for many of the men who already live on the edge of life. Their gang boss is bribing the prison bosses to keep them off this assignment. Another undermining element is the bread ration. Ivan overhears that it's been cut today. Survival becomes a little more challenging.

After a breakfast of gruel and boiled fish bones, Ivan goes to the infirmary where Nikolay Semyonovich Vdovushkin, the supposed medic, is writing poetry. Vdovushkin takes Ivan's temperature. It's ninety-nine degrees, not high enough to be admitted, so Ivan is sent off to work. Besides, Vdovushkin's patron, the new doctor, Stepan Grigoryevich, believes work is the best cure. But Ivan knows even a horse can die from overwork.

Ivan returns to the barracks and receives his bread ration, which is short. He eats half, then hides the rest in his mattress, sewing it in, in case the guards check for hidden items. As Ivan's gang stands outside waiting to be searched, Caesar Markovich, the rich intellectual who receives two packages a month, is smoking. Both Ivan and the scrounger Fetyukov watch him, hoping he'll pass the butt their way. Ivan waits with a semblance of self-control while Fetyukov hovers around like a dog. Caesar gives the butt to Ivan. This is another rule of prison survival: don't lose your dignity. Ivan goes to get his identification tag, S-984, repainted on his cap, chest, knee, and back, and the importance of dignity becomes clearer. The men's identities have been reduced to a letter and some numbers.

The feared Lieutenant Volkovoy supervises the frisk—despite the freezing cold—for non-regulation clothing or food, which might indicate an escape attempt. Captain Buynovsky, a newcomer, is caught with a jersey. He protests that this procedure violates Soviet law and is given ten days in solitary confinement. This means a hot meal only once every three days and a cut in bread rations and could easily mean death.

> "The big, red sun,… was slanting
> through the wires of the gate …"

As the gang heads to their old work place, thanks to the gang boss bribing their way out of the new and dreaded site, Ivan thinks of his wife and the *kolkhoz* or collective farm they lived on. She wants him to come back and paint carpets since most of the farmers are finding better incomes outside the farm. But, of course, he can't go home. He has been exiled from home.

When the gang arrives at the site to wait for their assignment, Ivan has a chance to think and observe his fellow gang members. He wonders how

Aloysha the Baptist can survive on only the prison rations: religious faith is barely tolerated in the atheist Soviet Union. He likes the minorities and the cultural qualities they bring. He likes the deaf prisoner, Senka Klevshin, who has already survived Buchenwald as a prisoner of World War II. Because of Article 58 of the penal code, Klevshin was given a ten-year sentence for "allowing" himself to become a prisoner of war and, therefore, spying for the enemy. Finally the men's assignments come and the work begins.

Ivan is to work with another Ivan, the Latvian. Since the quantity of work they do is tied to their food rations, there is sufficient motivation. For most of the men, losing themselves in work is their best escape. Still, the mind can wander. Ivan recalls how he came to the camps. Like Senka Klevshin, he too was captured by the Germans, but he escaped to rejoin his regiment, violating Article 58. Only those who consistently won battles or who died evaded Article 58.

The men are so busy working that they are late for their lunch of groats. Their portions are always reduced by other prisoners, especially those in the kitchen. However, the gang boss and his assistant always get double portions. The clever Ivan shows Pavlo, the assistant boss, two extra portions he's managed to steal. Pavlo lets Ivan have one and shows his humanity by giving the Captain the other.

Ivan overhears a debate about art between Caesar and prisoner K-123. Caesar praises the Eisenstein film *Ivan the Terrible* for its artistic merits while K-123 criticizes any artist who bends himself to the political regime, in this case, Stalin's. All art is a sore point in the Soviet Union, where freedom is not a value. The prime value is following the Communist party line.

Before the men return to work, they listen to Tyurin tell his story of imprisonment. His father was a *kulak* who resisted the collective farms. Because of this Tyurin was dishonorably discharged from the army and eventually arrested. Before his arrest, he took his younger brother to a street gang and asked them to show him how to survive. Even outside prison, the common Soviet citizen is forced to live like a criminal.

Tyurin tells the men to begin work and the most exhilarating part of the day takes place. Ivan lays bricks and is proud of the results. The men are late to return and have to be subjected to several counts, since the guards themselves could be imprisoned if they lost a man. The missing man is finally discovered, a Moldavian who fell asleep at his worksite. Although he is remorseful, he is sent to solitary confinement.

"The moon was really shining bright."

The rest of Ivan's day consists of earning more food by holding a place in the package line for Caesar, fighting his way past the orderly Clubfoot to get to his dinner, and buying tobacco with money he has made from odd jobs. He even gets Caesar's extra bread ration. Before roll call, Ivan feels pity for Fetyukov, who was beaten up for scrounging. He knows Fetyukov won't survive. He also feels sorry for Caesar, who might have most of the food from his package stolen, so he shows him how to hide it. The men are counted again before lights out. Caesar gives Ivan some of his goodies as thanks and Ivan shares with Aloysha. In bed Ivan hears Aloysha thank God and Ivan reviews his day, concluding that it was an unusually good one.

Characters

Alyoshka

Ivan's bunk mate, he is known by his religion. He represents the spiritual element that survives despite the atheism that is a cornerstone of Communism, in which the State is the only religion. He reads his Bible and is protected by Ivan, who respects his faith. In fact, Ivan wonders how Alyoshka can survive without extra rations and shares his cookie from Caesar with him.

The Baptist

See Alyoshka

Big Ivan

A tall, thin guard, he is the most easygoing of the lot.

Buynovsky

One of Ivan's bunk mates.

Captain Buynovsky

In the Russian navy, he was once a liaison officer on a British ship, since the British and

Russians were allies during World War II. But after receiving a thank-you gift from a British officer for his good service, he was sentenced to twenty-five years of hard labor. Throughout the novel he changes from a die-hard military man to a clever inmate. When Buynovsky is sentenced to face ten days in solitary confinement for insubordination, Ivan wonders whether he will survive.

Clubfoot

As his name implies, he is handicapped, but uses his disability to secure a good job. He's as hardboiled as anyone can be and even earns enough money to pay an assistant.

Der

The foreman at the construction site, he treats his fellow prisoners badly, but Ivan's gang sticks together against him to keep him in check.

Estonians

These two seem like brothers although they first met in camp; both are tall, fair, and thin and sleep in the same bunk. One of the two, called Eino, fills Ivan's request for tobacco after first consulting with his best friend.

Fetyukov

A scavenger whom Ivan dislikes. He used to be

a big shot in an office, but in prison he is beaten up for scrounging. In the end Ivan feels sorry for him.

Gopchik

Only sixteen years old, he is enthusiastic and alert. Ivan thinks he will go far in the camps. Ivan lost his own son and seems to have fatherly feelings for Gopchik.

Stepan Grigoryevich

Although new, he is already known as a loudmouth, know-it-all doctor who believes work is the best cure for illness.

Ivan Kilgas

A Latvian and former bricklayer, he receives two packages a month, speaks Russian like a native, and jokes most of the time. He works well with Ivan, who realizes he has more in common with the Latvian than with his own family.

Senka Klevshin

A little deaf, the former Buchenwald inmate says if you fussed there, you were finished. Ivan works with him and respects him as a fellow survivor.

Kuzyomin

An old gang boss of Ivan's, he tells his men that the law of the jungle prevails in prison: the only way to survive is to not lick your bowl clean, not count on the infirmary, and not betray or "squeal on" other prisoners. Ivan took his advice to heart and never forgot it.

Caesar Markovich

Caesar was a cinematographer before his imprisonment. A rich intellectual, he receives packages that keep him well fed, yet he shares his food. Art is his god.

Moldavian

He falls asleep in a warm corner during the work day and fails to turn up for the count. When finally discovered, he is extremely remorseful but is nevertheless taken to solitary confinement, where rations are eight ounces of bread a day and a hot meal every third day. Shukhov says that after ten days in solitary, a man would be so weakened that he would have a difficult time getting back on his feet again.

Panteleyev

The man missing from the gang: no one knows if he is sick or a squealer.

Pavlo

The assistant gang boss from West Ukrainia, which was under Poland until after World War II and where the people are still polite, unlike the typical Soviet.

Shkuropatenko

Of beanpole physique, he is a prisoner paid to guard prefabricated panels against the prisoners pilfering them.

Ivan Denisovich Shukhov

The main character, Ivan is a peasant who was drafted during World War II. He managed to escape a German prison camp and return to Russia. For this he was imprisoned, since Soviet law considered any escapee a spy for the Germans. Although Ivan was innocent he thought it wiser to plead guilty, knowing that if he pleaded innocent, he'd be shot, but if he pleaded guilty, he'd go to prison. Ivan is forty years old, balding, and missing half his teeth. Although he'll do everything he can to survive, he maintains a strict personal code. For example, he will never take or give a bribe, betray others, or lick his bowl clean. He represents the common man in the Soviet Union, an inspiring Russian survivor.

Thin Tartar

Called by his nationality, he is one of the guards, thin and hairless, who threatens to send Ivan to solitary confinement but then relents and sends him to mop the warders' office. The cold doesn't seem to bother him.

Tyurin

On his second sentence, this gang boss does everything he can to take care of the gang. Ivan knew him at another camp but wasn't in his gang. Of all the men in the camp, Tyurin is the one man Ivan would never cheat; the gang boss is crucial to survival.

Nikolay Semyonovich Vdovushkin

Technically a medic, he spends the day writing poetry, thanks to Dr. Grigoryevich, his patron. The Russian love for poetry is evident here.

Lieutenant Volkovoy

A much-feared disciplinary officer with a reputation for using a whip. His name is derived from "wolf."

Y-81

An old prisoner who has survived with his dignity intact, he is Ivan's hero.

Man versus Society

Ivan represents the common man; the immediate society he lives in is prison. Every day he struggles to survive physically and psychologically. The prison supplies him with the bare necessities: food, shelter, and a job. His choices are few, but the one great choice is his: to live or to die. His choice to survive impacts the greater society: man can go on despite whatever cruelties society imposes.

Media Adaptations

- *One Word of Truth* in videocassette form is a documentary narrated by Tom Courtney and produced by

Anglo-Nordic Productions that recreates Solzhenitsyn's Nobel Prize speech.

- Caspar Wrede filmed *One Day in the Life of Ivan Denisovich*, starring Tom Courtney.

- Alexander Ford adapted *The First Circle*, considered by many the most autobiographical of Solzhenitsyn's novels, for film in 1973.

The Truth versus the Lie

Ivan was imprisoned in the forced labor camp for the crime of high treason. During World War II, the Germans captured a great many Soviet soldiers. Ivan was one. However, he escaped and returned to his own lines. The Soviets believed he lied about escaping and was really spying for the Germans. Ivan realized if he told the truth, he'd be shot, but if he lied and said he was a spy, he'd be sent to prison. When one lie is stacked upon another, the light of truth is obscured. This is what happened under the tyranny of Josef Stalin, the Soviet leader—the vast majority of the Soviet people became accomplices to lies.

Life versus Death

Ivan chose living with lies over dying for truth. In his case, was the truth worth dying for or was surviving the better choice? What is the value of life and the value of the life Ivan is living? When is death of more value?

Good versus Evil

Every choice Ivan makes in his day is a moral one and is motivated by survival. He commits himself to his own survival by choosing to conserve his energy on a job that he doesn't want to do (mopping the floor for the inhuman warders) or to expand his energy on a job that gives him pleasure (bricklaying with the gang). He chooses who among the others should survive by selecting those who will receive his extra cookie or cigarette butt. His decision is always for the needy (for example, Alyoshka) instead of the greedy (Fetyukov).

The Individual versus the Unjust Law

In ancient Greece, Sophocles asked in his play *Antigone*, how does an individual deal with an unjust law? Should it be obeyed or flouted? To flout it one must be dedicated to a higher moral truth and one must be courageous. But in Ivan's world, this question is broader: how does an individual deal with an unjust system? Ivan gives his answer: survive it.

On Translations

Most critics feel the best of the original translations of *One Day in the Life of Ivan Denisovich* is the Bantam book version. According to the translators, Max Haywood and Ronald Hingley, Solzhenitsyn's novella is written in the slang from the concentration camp and in the vocabulary of the Russian peasant. To express this in English, they have used American slang, such as "can" and "cooler" for solitary confinement, and unpolished diction in expressions like "Let em through" and "Get outa the way." Russian obscenities, never before printed in the Soviet Union, were for the most part translated into their English equivalents.

The Novella

A novella is longer than a short story but shorter than a traditional novel. In *One Day*, Solzhenitsyn presents his tale like a long short story. There are no chapters, only a flowing narrative. The visual breaks are the spacings signaling a change of place or a change of time. This form also suggests that the reader can finish the work in one sitting to get its full impact.

Topics for Further Study

- During the 1940s and '50s, a practice called "blacklisting" took effect in the film industry in Hollywood. Any writer, director, or actor who had previously belonged to the Communist party could not find work. Investigate this reactionary stage of American history and examine it from all sides: the government prosecutors, the accused, the informants, and the sympathizers.

- The word "Siberia" conjures up a vision of an endless snowcovered plain and cold blue sky. Make a map of the camp Solzhenitsyn describes and plan an escape. Then, using a real map, choose a place in Siberia where the camp might have been located and plan an escape route out of the former USSR to freedom.

- Compare and contrast capitalism and communism. Remember that capitalism needs a free-market society in order to operate. How does each philosophy regard man, how does it effect the resulting culture, and what are the economic pluses and minuses of each?

- Find copies of *One Day in the Life of Ivan Denisovich* by different translators and compare a section of text that could suggest subtle but slightly different interpretations. Discuss and demonstrate the problems of studying literature in translation.

Socialist Realism

Literature under the Communists had to meet the standards of Socialist Realism; this meant not criticizing the Communist party. Therefore, content was more important than style, and since the party believed that religion was the "opiate of the people," that capitalism was evil, and that socialism was superior to all other political systems, content was severely limited. Writings resulted in contradictions, hypocracies, and lies: "victory without defeat, radical social change without injustice, and complete centralization of power without autocracy," according to James Curtis in *Solzhenitsyn's Traditional Imagination.*

Point of View

Solzhenitsyn uses the third person, limited omniscient narrator. This means the story is told by a narrator who refers to all the characters as he, she, or they and describes the thoughts and feelings of the main character, in this case, Ivan. Therefore, the narrator is omniscient or all-knowing with regard to Ivan. However, he is limited with regard to the other characters who are only described externally, not internally. The third person allows the narrator to make general comments outside of the main character's mind. For example: "But now all at once something happened in the column, like a wave going through it.... The fellows in the back—that's where Shukhov was—had to run now ..."

Chekhovian Technique

Christopher Moody in *Solzhenitsyn* points out that Solzhenitsyn uses Chekhov's technique of "evoking a whole impression by means of a few ... emotionally neutral" words. For example, from the very beginning of the book, the cold is mentioned as is the value of footwear, so by the time Ivan leaves with his gang for the outside and "the snow creaked under their boots," the complete setting of the pre-dawn, freezing cold in a stark, snowflattened landscape comes alive. The creaking is the warning sound that less than an inch of boot separates flesh from ice, and therefore life from death …

Russian Terms

There are a few terms used in the novella that are strictly Russian. *Zek* refers to a man serving in a forced-labor camp or one who has already served. The "free workers" are former zeks who have nowhere to go, so they work for the camp. *Kolkhozniks* are collective farmers and a *kolkhoz* is a collective farm. *Kulaks* are displaced farmers who rejected the collective farms.

Censorship in Russian Literature

The history of Russian literature has been one of censorship, first under the czars and then under the Soviets. In the 19th century, the poet Pushkin, the novelists Turgenev, Tolstoy and Dostoyevski, and the dramatists Gogol and Chekhov, to name a few, elevated Russian literature to world renown, but these writers labored under the threat of exile, imprisonment, or death if their works were deemed politically unacceptable. Pushkin was exiled for a time. Dostoyevski had a crueler experience: he was condemned to the firing squad before the czar's messenger brought the order to commute the execution at the very last minute. In the 20th century, under the Soviets, censorship seemed even more severe and difficult to contain under the explosive advances of mass communication. But the Soviets felt that if communism wasn't the practical solution to all social ills, they would not allow that failing to come to the attention of the outside world. Soviet writers were forbidden to criticize the system; if they dared, they were silenced. A great writer like Bulgakov had his works banned, while the Nobel prize-winning Pasternak had his works smuggled out of the country to be published in the West.

Compare & Contrast

- **1914:** Russia enters World War I against Germany and Austria-Hungary, enduring several crushing defeats.

- **1917:** The Russian Revolution refers to two revolutions. In March, starving rioters joined by the army overthrow the Romanov czars who ruled Russia for over three hundred years. In October, a second revolution led by Lenin put the Bolsheviks in power.

- **1918–20:** Russia pulls out of World War I.

- **1932–34:** Famine results from agricultural collectivization (communal farming); the government conceals this from the outside world so that no international aid can come to alleviate the situation. Cannibalism is rampant in the countryside and starving villagers attack nearby villages for food. Roughly 10 to 15 million people perish in the famine and the epidemics that follow.

- **1929–38:** Stalin purges the party of his enemies and supposed enemies; by 1937, he begins to purge the Red

Army, resulting in millions of citizens being arrested and sentenced to the camps. (Anyone arrested has their family, friends and associates arrested; this accounts for every Soviet citizen having some personal involvement with the camps); by 1938 the Red Army, having lost its trained officers, is considerably weakened.

- **1941:** Stalin is considered responsible for the demoralization and decimation of the Red Army. Officers are shot if they refuse to lead impossible missions and soldiers who were captured by the German enemy and escaped are punished. Their families feel the consequences also. The Red Army is guessed to have lost 7 to 10 million men in the course of World War II according to J.N. Westwood in *Russia:1917–1964*.

- **1942:** In the Battle of Stalingrad the Russians valiantly defeat the Germans, resulting in a turning point of World War II.

- **1945:** World War II ends and the Soviets begin accumulating 6 satellite countries of Eastern Europe.

- **1953:** Stalin dies.

- **1922–91:** The Union of Soviet Socialist Republics is created and becomes the most powerful Communist nation on earth. The USSR finally collapses, the satellite countries Russia dominated claim their independence, and Russia, too, becomes an independent nation again.

The Penal Camps

One hundred years after Dostoyevski wrote *Notes from the House of the Dead* about his experiences in a penal camp, Solzhenitsyn wrote *One Day in the Life of Ivan Denisovich*. According to critic Christopher Moody in *Solzhenitsyn*, after one hundred years the penal camps had become even more inhumane. In Dostoyevski's time, prisoners received sufficient food, enough time to devote to private activities, the opportunity to socialize with the nearby population, and the "certain knowledge of freedom at the end of their term." Solzhenitsyn's prisoners had no such guarantee. In fact, once free, they were exiled from their home towns.

Josef Stalin

The question arises: what happened in those hundred years to worsen things to such an inhumane degree? In a word, Stalin. Josef Stalin also spent time in these camps, but he was a man dedicated to political ideology. He clawed his way to the position of dictator over the bodies of his competitors, ruthlessly formed the Soviet Union into a world power, and earned the reputation of being perhaps the greatest mass murderer in Western civilization. Although Solzhenitsyn refers only once to Stalin in his novella, the ruler's demonic spirit permeates the camp. The paranoid laws that condemned so many of the men to camp were the same laws that condemned any real freedom outside of it.

Nikita Khrushchev

In 1950, Nikita Khrushchev, then premier of the USSR, wanted to de-Stalinize the Communist Party. He attributed the fact that Josef Stalin had destroyed more Soviet people than those who died in all Russian wars combined and yet retained his incredible hold over the Soviet people to "the cult of personality." Khrushchev wanted to put an end to Stalin's influence beyond the grave in order to strengthen his own power, and Solzhenitsyn's story seemed the perfect eulogy. Thanks to Solzhenitsyn's courage and continuing novels, the truth about Stalin was destined to live.

Critical Overview

Although Solzhenitsyn's work deals with politics from *One Day in the Life of Ivan Denisovich* to *The Gulag Archipelago*, perhaps what has been most detrimental to his reputation is his political statements. After being expelled from the Soviet Union and seeking refuge in Europe and the United States, he constantly criticized the West. Invited to give the commencement speech at Harvard University, Solzhenitsyn attracted one of the largest crowds in Harvard's history and was televised nationally. In his address, entitled "The World Split Apart," he called for unification, but his remarks seemed to create new splits and his speech was highly criticized.

Solzhenitsyn is a mathematician and physicist by training and a writer by profession. When asked to speak, however, he inevitably poses questions on politics and philosophy and freely gives his own answers. Although many of his criticisms are valid, he has a xenophobic vision of Russia, seeing it as morally superior to the West because Russia skipped the stage of competitive capitalism on her way to cooperative socialism. Many critics also believe that he misunderstands the inherent duality of western freedom, that it results in bad choices as well as good ones. Michael Scammell in *Solzhenitsyn: A Biography* quotes Solzhenitsyn as saying, "I cannot be regarded in political terms. A writer's view differs in kind from that of the politician or the philosopher." Yet, as Scammell concludes, Solzhenitsyn chooses not to take the stance of the writer, but instead embraces that of the political philosopher.

Solzhenitsyn's moral integrity remains unquestioned, his literary skills are laudable even in poor translations, and he is often forgiven much politicizing because he comes from the literary tradition of socialist realism. While his intellectual sweep is not generally considered all-encompassing, most critics do not expect it to be.

Sources

David Burg, and George Feifer, *Solzhenitsyn*, Stein and Day Publishers, pp. 155-156.

James M. Curtis, *Solzhenitsyn's Traditional Imagination*, The University of Georgia Press, 1984, p. 185.

Max Hayward and Ronald Hingley, translators, *One Day in the Life of Ivan Denisovich*, Bantam Books, 1963, p. xviii.

Christopher Moody, *Solzhenitsyn*, Barnes and Noble, 1976, pp. 37-38.

Michael Scammell, *Solzhenitsyn: A Biography*, Norton, p. 981.

J. N. Westwood, *Russia 1917–1964*, Harper & Row, 1966, p. 122.

For Further Study

Steven Allaback, *Alexander Solzhenitsyn*, Taplinger Publishing Company, 1978.

> An informative look at the craftsmanship and genius of *One Day in the Life of Ivan Denisovich, The First Circle, The Cancer Ward*, and *August 1914*.

Francis Barker, *Solzhenitsyn: Politics and Form*, Barnes & Noble, 1977.

> The author traces Solzhenitsyn's rejection of Marxism and a willingness to explore democracy in his first novels to a reactionary political vision in his later ones.

Ronald Berman, editor, *Solzhenitsyn at Harvard*, Ethics and Public Policy Center, 1980.

> Solzhenitsyn's famous commencement address at Harvard is reprinted, followed by media comments and essays for a deeper analysis of that event.

Hans Bjorkegren, *Aleksandr Solzhenitsyn: A Biography*, The Third Press, 1972.

> Translated from the Swedish, this biography has the insight expected from an ever-vigilant neighbor.

Olga Carlisle, *Solzhenitsyn and the Secret Circle*, Holt, Rinehart and Winston, 1978.

> Born in Russia, American by marriage, and an enemy of Solzhenitsyn's, Olga Carlisle presents her assertion that she and her husband, a translator, were used by Solzhenitsyn.

Alex De Jonge, *Stalin and the Shaping of the Soviet Union*, William Morrow and Company, Inc., 1986.

> De Jonge used archival material and living witnesses to trace Stalin's humble beginnings and his rise to despotism, his purges and liquidations, his role in World War II, and the subsequent expanding of the USSR map.

Helene Carrere D'Encausse, *Stalin: Order through Terror*, Longman, 1981.

> In her second volume on the history of the Soviet Union, this Parisian professor examines the rise of Stalinism until Stalin's death.

John B. Dunlop, Richard Haugh, and Alexis Klimoff, editors, *Aleksandr Solzhenitsyn: Critical Essays and Documentary Materials*, Nordland Publishing, 1973.

> This volume includes not only literary criticism of Solzhenitsyn in English but also four translated

> documents written by Solzhenitsyn
> about his philosophy and his craft.

John B. Dunlop, Richard S. Haugh, and Michael Nicholson, editors, *Solzhenitsyn in Exile*, Hoover Institution Press, 1985.

> A collection of essays and documentary material of particular use to researchers. The critical essays examine Solzhenitsyn and his work; the documentary material consists of memoirs, interviews, and bibliographies.

John and Carol Gerrard, *Inside the Soviet Writers' Union*, Collier Macmillan, 1990.

> The authors look inside one of the Soviet Union's most powerful tools for propaganda, the Writers' Union. Dedicated to the idea of Socialist Realism, this organization did its best to kill Russian creativity.

Paul Gray, "Russia's Prophet in Exile," *Time*, Vol. 134, No. 4, July 24, 1989, pp. 56-60.

> An insightful interview with Solzhenitsyn on politics, literature, and religion.

Oakley Hall, *The Art & Craft of Novel Writing*, Writer's Digest Books, 1989.

> Not only is this a well-thought analysis of how to write a novel, but it explains the techniques that lead

the reader to the desired response.

K. P., "The Sage of Vermont," *Forbes*, Vol. 153, No. 10, May 9, 1994, p. 122.

A brief, unbiased overview of Solzhenitsyn's relationship to the United States.

Nikita S. Khrushchev, *Khrushchev Remembers: The Last Testament*, Little, Brown and Company, 1974.

The last volume of an oral history dictated by the former premier has a fascinating section on Stalin and his treatment of writers.

Vladislav Krasnov, *Solzhenitsyn and Dostoevsky*, University of Georgia Press, 1980.

Using the three earliest Solzhenitsyn novels, the author states that Solzhenitsyn is closer to Dostoevsky than Tolstoy, especially in the concept of the polyphonic novel where there is no main character, but rather several.

Georg Lukacs, *Solzhenitsyn*, The MIT Press, 1969.

A literary criticism that judges Solzhenitsyn in the tradition of Socialist Realism and the literary problems of the Stalinist era.

Judith Newman, "From Vermont, with Love," *People*, Vol. 41, No. 18, May 16, 1994, pp. 99-102.

The people of Vermont give a fond

good-bye to the Solzhenitsyn family.

"Profile of Aleksandr Solzhenitsyn," *1988 Current Biography Yearbook*, H. W. Wilson Company, 1988.

> A comprehensive sketch of the author which highlights milestones in his life and is accompanied by his photographs.

Edvard Radzinsky, *Stalin: The First In-Depth Biography Based On Explosive New Documents from Russia's Secret Archives*, Doubleday, 1996.

> This very readable translation by H. T. Willetts of the life of Stalin is organized into three sections: one for each of Stalin's names (his childhood name, the teenage name he gives himself, and the name of Stalin, meaning "steel"). Each chapter is divided into subtitled sections.

Abraham Rothberg, *Aleksandr Solzhenitsyn: The Major Novels*, Cornell University Press, 1971.

> An analysis of Solzhenitsyn's first three novels, this critique reaffirms the importance of the works from a moral, political, and artistic standpoint.

Marshall D Shulman, *Stalin's Foreign Policy Reappraised*, Harvard University Press, 1963.

> A scholar of international politics, Shulman argues, contrary to popular

opinion, that Russia's foreign policy began to become more flexible even before the death of Stalin.

Aleksandr Solzhenitsyn, *August 1914*, Farrar, Straus and Giroux, 1971.

This polyphonic novel examines the Battle of Tannenberg in World War I, a Russian defeat that showed the corruptions of the czarist system.

Aleksandr Solzhenitsyn, *Candle in the Wind*, University of Minnesota Press, 1960.

A play that examines scientific ethics: a scientist is confronted by a woman whose personality has been changed by biofeedback techniques.

Aleksandr Solzhenitsyn, *From under the Rubble*, Little, Brown and Company, 1974.

This collection of essays, edited by Solzhenitsyn and including two of his own essays, seeks to find a new, moral society. Soviet Russia is severely criticized and the West is seen as decadent.

Aleksandr Solzhenitsyn, *The Gulag Archipelago*, Harper & Row, 1973.

The "Gulag" is the acronym of secret police organizations including the camps. The author indicts this insidious segment of Soviet life using hundreds of characters and their stories.

Aleksandr Solzhenitsyn, *Lenin in Zurich*, Farrar, Straus and Giroux, 1975.

> Chapters on Lenin in *August 1914*, Knot I, and in Knots II and III have now been enlarged and presented as a separate book, thanks to valuable research material Solzhenitsyn found in Zurich.

Aleksandr Solzhenitsyn, *Letter to the Soviet Leaders*, Harper & Row, 1974.

> In "Nothing Changes for the Good," Solzhenitsyn predicts the destruction of Russia and the West. "War with China" is also a fascinating chapter and a cautionary tale for any country.

Aleksandr Solzhenitsyn, *The Oak and The Calf*, Harper & Row, 1979.

> Solzhenitsyn's memoir of his writing career in Russia and how he had to confront even the KGB, the secret police. This English-language version, published four years after the Russian one, has added material.

Aleksandr Solzhenitsyn, *Solzhenitsyn: A Pictorial Autobiography*, Farrar, Straus and Giroux, 1974.

> Solzhenitsyn has put together a book of snapshots, most of which are of him. The writing is a short and powerful recapping of his life under

Soviet tyranny.

Aleksandr Solzhenitsyn, *Warning to the West*, Farrar, Straus and Giroux, 1976.

> Solzhenitsyn begs the West to intervene in Soviet affairs for the future of the world.

B. H. Sumner, *A Short History of Russia*, Harcourt, Brace & World, Inc., 1949.

> As the title implies, this is a brief overview of Russia divided into the following components: the frontier, the state, the land, the church, the Slavs, the sea, and the West.